JANET GUTHRIE

JANET GUTHRIE
First Woman Driver
At Indianapolis

EDWARD F. DOLAN, Jr.
AND RICHARD B. LYTTLE

Doubleday & Company, Inc.
Garden City, New York

Library of Congress Cataloging in Publication Data
Dolan, Edward F 1924–
    Janet Guthrie, first woman driver at Indianapolis.
    (A Signal book)
    Includes index.
    SUMMARY: A biography of the physicist who broke
into the all-male world of the Indianapolis 500.
    1. Guthrie, Janet, 1938–   —Juvenile literature.
2. Automobile racing drivers—United States—Biography
—Juvenile literature.   3. Indianapolis Speedway Race—
Juvenile literature.   [1. Guthrie, Janet, 1938–
2. Automobile racing drivers]   I. Lyttle, Richard B.,
joint author.   II. Title.
GV1032.G87D64   796.7′2′0924   [B]   [92]
ISBN 0-385-12526-7 Trade
Library of Congress Catalog Card Number 77–12848

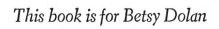

This book is for Betsy Dolan

For their help in the preparation of this book, our thanks go to Al Bloemker of the Indianapolis Motor Speedway, Roger Brady of Leyland Motor Sales, Inc., and Arthur N. Orthun of Carl Byoir & Associates, Inc. And a very special word of appreciation to Leonard F. Marino, vice-president, Macmillan Ring-Free Oil Company, Inc., for all his kind assistance.

CONTENTS

JANET GUTHRIE

1

First Woman at Indy

The *Bryant Special* flashed past the grandstand at the Indianapolis Motor Speedway and headed into the curve at the end of the straightaway. Low-slung, wide-tired, and painted blue, it rode up close to the concrete wall bordering the track. Then it shot into the far straightaway.

More than 50,000 fans in the grandstand and the infield area listened to the roar of its Offenhauser engine. They liked the sound, crackling and deep in the spring air. The *Bryant Special*, almost a blur as it hit 152 miles per hour on the far straightaway, was zooming through a practice run and looking good.

"Stand on it!" the crowd shouted to the driver. They wanted more speed with every turn of the wheels. The car was doing just fine, yes. But, one of these days soon, it would have to go a lot faster if it hoped to win a starting spot in the biggest and most exciting racing event in the United States—the annual Indianapolis 500.

The sixtieth running of the Indy classic was scheduled for Sunday, May 30, 1976, a little more than two weeks from now. Every fan who came out to watch the daily practice sessions knew that seventy-one of the world's top drivers had assembled here at the famous "Brickyard" outside Indianapolis, Indiana, to climb into their cars and try to qualify for the 500-miler. But only the fastest thirty-three cars would make it. For a very particular reason, the fans wanted the *Bryant Special* to be among the lucky thirty-three.

Yes, that 743-horsepower Offy was sounding good.

"Keep it up!"

"Go!"

"Stand on it!"

But, at the wheel, the driver was frowning and leaning forward against the safety straps. Something had gone wrong. Above the roar of the engine and the wind, the driver could hear a strange grinding noise. It was coming from up front and over on the right.

A wheel bearing. From the sound, it was giving out.

The driver eased back on the accelerator. The crowd groaned as the *Special* suddenly lost speed, glided through a curve, and coasted along the straightaway in front of the grandstand. The driver angled off the track and nosed into the pit area. Mechanics in oil-stained coveralls ran to meet the car. It braked to a stop.

The groan of the crowd changed to an excited buzzing. Spectators began asking each other, "What's wrong now?" The *Special* had been having trouble ever since its arrival down in Gasoline Alley a few days ago. There had been one problem after another, with a couple of burned pistons, a broken oil line, and a bad clutch hub leading the list. Now, just as it was getting its tires warmed up after a few good practice laps, the *Special* was in trouble again.

As the mechanics surrounded the car, the driver undid the chin strap on the crash helmet. Up went the face mask. There were a few quick words. A gloved hand pointed toward the right front wheel.

Nodding, the mechanics quickly got to work. The driver climbed out and stood watching them—and now it was very clear why all the fans wanted the *Special* to qualify for the 500. The driver was wearing a bulky driving suit, but it couldn't hide the fact that it covered a narrow-waisted figure. Then off came the helmet. Then the asbestos hood that covered the head and stretched across the chin. And there for all to see were the soft features of the face. The driver was a young woman.

Her name was Janet Guthrie. She was a slender woman, standing five feet nine inches tall and weighing 135 pounds. Blondish hair, parted over on the right, fell in waves almost to her shoulders. Her eyes were wide-spaced and a penetrating light blue. Her expression was serious now, but when she smiled, it was a wide and friendly smile.

The name Janet was printed in bold letters on the

3

side of her helmet. She stood now, with the helmet cradled in one arm, and all eyes in the grandstand were on her. Everyone knew that this trim-figured driver was trying to make history here at Indianapolis.

She was out to crack the world of big-car racing and become the first woman ever to compete in the 500.

But could she do it?

That question was bringing out thousands of fans each day to watch the practice runs. They all wanted a glimpse of her at the wheel. If only she could qualify, they thought. Then they would see one of the most re-markable Indy races of all time.

In making her bid, Janet was trying to add her name to a list of the century's greatest drivers. Almost every-one in the stands could have talked for hours about them. About Ray Harroun and his zippy Marmon *Wasp* taking the first 500 way back in 1911. About Gaston Chevrolet and Frank Lockhart in the 1920s. About Louis Mayer and Wilbur Shaw in the 1930s. Mauri Rose and Bill Vukovich in the '40s and '50s. And Par-nelli Jones, A. J. Foyt, Mario Andretti, Al Unser, and Johnny Rutherford in the '60s and '70s.

Now wouldn't it be something if Janet Guthrie could add her name to that list?

To many, the idea seemed impossible. Close to two thousand drivers had battled it out in the 500 over the years, and not one of them had been a woman. Why, until just two years ago women hadn't even been al-lowed to visit the pit area. Indy was a tough world. An

4

oily world full of the roar of engines. A man's world. Completely.

In this man's world, it had long been said that no woman could ever handle the big Indy cars. Championship cars, they were called. Weighing about 1,500 pounds, they were open-cockpit, rear-engine, turbocharged jobs. Cars with so much horsepower that they zoomed along like earthbound rockets. Women drivers just didn't have the strength, the skill, or the experience to get them around the track.

At least, that's what had always been said.

But everything was going to go right out the window if Janet made it to the 500. She'd prove that all the talk had been wrong. She'd open the way for more women drivers, and the world of Indy would never be the same again.

Until two months before, most of the big-car fans in the crowd had never heard of Janet Guthrie. Only those spectators who followed sports car racing knew her name. In the past thirteen years she had competed in more than 120 sports car races at such great tracks as Sebring, Daytona, Watkins Glen, and Bridgehampton. To people in the know, she had the reputation of being one of the best women drivers in the country. But her name had been anything but a household word. Most sports car drivers don't get all the newspaper space that the big-car drivers do.

But life had changed completely for Janet last March when she had announced her plans to try for the 500.

5

She had never before raced in championship cars. They were three times as powerful as sports racers. But a big-car owner had hired her to go to Indy just the same. From then on, she was "news." The sports pages were full of her name. Now, indeed, the people in the stands knew all about her.

They knew that she was an intelligent woman. That she was a physicist and had once worked as an engineer in the aerospace industry. That she was single because her commitment to racing left little time for marriage and a home. That she liked to cook, listen to classical music, and attend the ballet. And even that the works of Shakespeare were to be found on the bookshelves in her apartment, right along with all her books on motor sports.

They knew also that she was a determined woman. You had to be determined if you hoped to be a driver. Some of her best races had been endurance runs. Twelve hours at Sebring. Twenty-four at Daytona. Determination is a must if you're to sit behind the wheel for all those hours, fighting off a growing tiredness as you grind out the miles.

But there was more to her than just determination. The fans had learned that she was also a quiet woman, soft-spoken, and modest. She openly admitted that she was inexperienced in championship cars but that she was working hard to learn. She didn't blow up when reporters asked if her bid for the 500 wasn't just a publicity stunt and tied in with the "women's lib" movement. She replied quietly that she wanted to be known not as a woman driver but as a driver who had come up from sports car racing.

And there was her sense of fun. Oh, she was very serious about the 500. Make no mistake about *that*. But still she bubbled with excitement about being here at Indy. And her smile was always wide whenever she recalled her first test run at the wheel of a championship car. She said it was like taking a ride to the moon.

But, most of all, the fans knew that she was proving herself able to handle the big championship cars. Soon after making her announcement, she had competed in her first Indy-type race—the Trenton 200 in New Jersey. She hadn't come in anywhere near first place, but she'd done a good job just the same. Her speed had been fine. She had driven carefully and expertly. Many of the men drivers who felt that a woman didn't belong in an Indy car had begun to change their minds about Janet Guthrie.

And so here she was—quiet, determined, and a good driver—watching the pit crew work on the *Special*. True to what she had said, a wheel bearing proved to be the problem. Once the trouble was fixed, she put on her helmet and dropped into the cockpit, ready to continue the practice run.

She knew that the people in the stands were watching her closely and that thousands everywhere were pulling for her to make the 500. She hoped that her car, bothered by one mechanical problem after another, wouldn't break down when the time came to qualify. And she hoped that *she* wouldn't break down and make some mistake that would disappoint everyone—herself included.

Whatever happened, Janet Guthrie knew that she would try her best. It's what a lifetime in racing had taught her to do.

2

The Road to Racing

The small plane flew high above the hospital at Iowa City, Iowa, on March 7, 1938. At the controls was William Lain Guthrie. Deftly, he put the plane through a series of stunts and then banked away toward the airport he operated on the outskirts of town. He was smiling broadly. The stunts had been his way of celebrating the birth of his daughter, Janet, far below.

Janet was the first of five children born to William and his wife. The child was to have few memories of Iowa City, for, when she was yet very small, the family moved to Florida. There, William flew as a captain for Eastern Airlines. Home for Janet became the sun-drenched city of Miami.

She grew steadily into a tallish, quiet girl who seemed little different from her playmates. But, in one way, Janet was different. The daughter of a flier, she early showed a streak of daring, a liking for adventure. It was a sign of the racing driver to come. She put it to use for one of the first times when she was just thirteen. She learned to fly a plane.

Her father was delighted with her interest in flying. And with how quickly she learned to handle the controls of a Piper Cub. But that streak of daring could also be pretty darned hair-raising at times.

This was particularly true when William and his wife heard their teen-age pilot announce that she now wanted to learn parachute jumping. They shook their heads with disapproval. Parachuting was too dangerous a business. They couldn't believe Janet was serious. But she was and she proved it when she was sixteen. One summer day, she climbed to the roof of the family's one-story home, took a deep breath, and leaped to a safe landing.

She tried her first real parachute jump a short time later.

Altogether, it was an exciting time for the Guthrie family because Janet also made her first solo flight when she was sixteen. She went on to earn a private pilot's license at seventeen, a commercial license at nineteen, and then an instructor's license. By the time she was twenty-one, Janet had logged more than 400 hours in the air and was able to handle at least twenty different types of plane.

Daring though she was, flying and parachuting were the chief adventures of Janet's teen years. Otherwise, her life was a quiet one, made up of daily classes, home-work, and parties. She attended Miss Harris' Florida

Janet Guthrie—first woman to try for the Indianapolis 500. (Photo courtesy Macmillan Ring-Free Oil Company)

It was in a Jaguar XK-120
that Janet began her
sports racing career.
She soon switched over to
a more powerful XK-140.
(Photo courtesy Leyland
Motor Sales, Inc.)

Janet posed for this
photograph soon after
joining the Macmillan
Motor Maids.
It became one of the best-
known photos ever taken
of her.
It was used to illustrate
newspaper stories,
racing programs, and
magazine articles.
(Photo courtesy Macmillan
Ring-Free Oil Company)

This is the Austin-Healy
prototype driven by Janet
at Sebring in 1969.
(Photo courtesy Macmillan
Ring-Free Oil Company)

Janet, Liane Engeman,
and Donna Mae Mims pose
with the KLG-Nisonger
Trophy that they won at
Sebring in 1969.
The race marked the
second time that the
Motor Maids took the
trophy, which is awarded
to the best all-girl team
in the competition.
(Photo courtesy Macmillan
Ring-Free Oil Company).

Janet discusses track and car
problems with a fellow driver just
before a twelve-hour run at Sebring.
She had a remarkable record in
endurance runs, building a string
of nine straight finishes by 1971.
(United Press
International Photo)

Janet poses for the camera in
the garage area at Sebring.
(Photo courtesy Macmillan
Ring-Free Oil Company)

The all-girl driving team made many public appearances on behalf of the Macmillan Company. Here, Janet and Liane Engeman sign in on a visit to the Forty-Seventh Tactical Fighter Squadron at McDill Air Force Base in Florida. Janet also went before the television cameras to talk of her life as a sports car driver. (Photo courtesy Macmillan Ring-Free Oil Company)

Janet poses with her
Toyota Celica.
Driving a Celica, she
also captured the North
American Road Racing
Championship in 1973.
(Photo courtesy Carl Byoir & Associates)

Janet and fellow driver,
Dick Simon.
Simon, an Indy veteran,
wasn't happy when he
learned that he was to
help prepare a woman
for the 500.
But he changed his mind
when he saw Janet make
her test runs at Ontario.
(Photo courtesy Indianapolis Motor
Speedway Corporation)

Sign of trouble to come? Janet tries to relax while her crewmen make some minor adjustments on the Bryant Special *during the practice runs for the Trentonian. The car performed well in the race itself, but then encountered one mechanical problem after another when Janet arrived at Indianapolis.* (United Press International Photo)

The famous "Brickyard"—the Indianapolis Motor Speedway. (Photo courtesy Indianapolis Motor Speedway Corporation)

School for Girls, a private school. Then, deeply interested in science, she went to study physics at the University of Michigan. She graduated with a Bachelor of Science degree.

Now it was time to put her skills as a physicist to work. She was offered a teaching position abroad—at the University of Lebanon—but took a job instead as an engineer with the Republic Aviation company in Long Island, New York. The year was 1960 and the United States was just setting out to send men to the moon. Janet found herself working on the development of suborbital and space vehicles. Fascinated by all that was going on, she stayed with Republic for six years. Then she went to the Sperry-Rand Corporation, where she edited technical publications.

In 1965, Janet's love for adventure showed itself again. NASA (the National Aeronautics and Space Administration) was in charge of America's efforts to reach the moon, and Janet heard that it was starting a program to train women astronauts. Space flight! That was for her! She immediately tried out and was one of the four women who passed the first series of tests for the program.

But she wasn't destined to rocket off into space. The officials in charge of the program decided that women astronauts must have Ph.D. degrees. These were very advanced degrees. Janet, who had only a Bachelor of Science degree, had to drop out.

But what about auto racing? When did it become a part of Janet's busy life?

11

Her mother once told a reporter that it all started back at Miss Harris' School. One day a friend of Janet's drove up in a sporty car. It was a Jaguar XK-120. Janet took one look at its sleek lines and right then and there made a promise to herself. The car was beautiful and she would have one just like it. As soon as she was earning her own money and had saved enough.

Janet kept her promise in 1962. The XK-120 was a used one, nine years old. But Janet was delighted with her purchase, with its six-cylinder engine, its leather seats, its sloping hood and curving fenders. But she quickly learned something about herself. She was good with planes, yes, but she didn't know a thing about cars. She knew so little, in fact, that she had to ask her ten-year-old brother how the clutch worked.

Then, soon after she had the XK-120 moving and was becoming accustomed to handling it, Janet learned something else. She had bought the car for its beauty, but now she found herself more interested in "what it could do." How well did it accelerate? How fast could it go? How did it corner? Before long, her test runs made the Jaguar one of the most familiar sights on the roads near the Republic Aviation plant.

Everything about the car won her over. She liked its speed, the rush of the wind against her face, and the feeling of mounting power as she went up through the gears. It was all a glorious adventure. Her first love, flying, gave way to a brand new love.

Soon, however, Janet was looking for something to do

with the Jaguar other than road test it. She became interested in the local sports car clubs and entered their gymkhana competitions. Gymkhanas are low-speed events that are meant to sharpen a new driver's skills at the wheel. Much like a skier on a slalom run, each contestant moves along a course marked with pylons, the idea being to drive a twisting path through the pylons without knocking a one over. The cars also participate in parking contests, seeing which driver can get neatly into a small space in the shortest time. Still other gymkhana events call for the driver to accelerate to around 30 mph and then stop with his wheels touching a line drawn on the ground.

Janet performed so well in these events that she was named the women's gymkhana champion of Long Island in 1962.

The gymkhanas did much to develop her driving skills. But, thorough young woman that she was, she wanted to be even better. Her aim was to handle the XK-120 as well as she handled a plane. And so she took time off from work and attended a driving school. It was held at the Lime Rock sports car track in Connecticut.

She proved to be a good student—so good, indeed, that she caught the eye of veteran driver Gordon McKenzie. He felt she was a natural at the wheel. She was both daring and careful. Her sense of timing was excellent. She was calm and quick-thinking in emergencies. McKenzie was so impressed that one day he approached Janet with a question.

Had she ever thought about becoming a sports car racing driver?

Janet blinked with surprise.

The idea was new to her. It was also one that was going to change her whole life.

3

Getting Started

Janet thought about Gordon McKenzie's suggestion for a time. Then she made her decision. Yes, it would be fun to be a sports car racing driver.

As soon as she began to talk about the sport with other drivers, she found that it was a fairly new one. It is true that flashy little sports cars had been around since the early days of the automobile and that their drivers had always enjoyed zipping them over the roads in informal races. But there had been few such drivers. And there had been little interest in their races. The sport had to wait until the mid-1940s before it began to catch on.

World War II was just ending and Janet had been just a little girl at the time. She hadn't known of the three things that started the sport on its way to popularity.

First, a group of seven men in the Boston area formed

the Sports Car Club of America (SCCA) to hold organized races across the country under a strict set of rules. Second, once the war ended, European sports cars began to be manufactured again. Compact and high-powered, they soon appeared in America. Car enthusiasts took one look at them and could hardly wait to see what they could do in a race.

Finally, out of all the European cars, there were two that really fired the imagination. Both came from England. They were the British MG-TC and the Jaguar XK-120.

Each in its own way was a great performer. The stubby MG wasn't too powerful—it could wind itself up to just 75 mph—but it handled beautifully and was nothing but fun to drive. As for the Jag—well, it could give you all the power and speed you needed. And, best of all, both were inexpensive. The MG cost around $2,400 and the XK-120 less than $4,000. People who had longed to try their hand at sports racing now saw a way to get in on all the action without spending a fortune.

There were organized races sponsored by a club and great cars. And two cars, the MG and the XK-120, that would-be drivers could afford. The sport was on its way.

The first races were something to see. The cars needed lots of room and wanted the challenge of twists and turns. The oval tracks used for midget and championship cars just wouldn't do. And so the drivers took to the open road. They zoomed along country lanes, up and down hills, and through city streets. One of the first

SCCA races was held at Watkins Glen in New York state, and the pit area was right in the middle of town—with stores on all sides.

Though those first races were as exciting as could be, they were also very dangerous. The spectators crowded right up to the road and sometimes dashed out in front of the oncoming cars to get from one side to another. If a car went out of control, it was apt to sail right into a group of onlookers or through someone's fence. And, if there was a crash, people had to run and duck pieces of flying machinery.

After a number of spectators had been injured, it was decided that the sport should be taken off public roads and given closed tracks of its own. But there was the problem of space. Since the cars needed so much room for long straightaways, bends, dips, rises, and various turns, the tracks would take up countless acres and cost millions to build. Impossible!

Then someone had an idea. How about all the airports that had been built for military purposes during World War II? They were no longer being used. Wouldn't they do for a start?

The answer was "yes." The racers would have all the room they needed, with plenty left over for the fans to watch in safety. Courses were immediately laid out on several airports across the country. Some of today's best known tracks—among them Sebring in Florida—started life as airfields. Then, as the sport ballooned in popularity, tracks not on airport grounds also began to take shape.

By the time Janet had bought her XK-120, sports car racing was well organized. More than seventy tracks dotted the country, with new ones being added almost every year. Participating were cars from all over the world. Some were passenger models that could also race. Others were modified for better performance and greater speed. And still others were built primarily for racing.

So that the competition would be fair, the cars battled it out according to "class." Each class was made up of models that were much the same in power and performance. Some races featured cars of just one class. Others allowed a number of classes to race at the same time. In these latter races, there were two kinds of winners—winners in class, and overall winners who came in ahead of everyone else. Avoided always was the unfairness of putting a little MG-TC and Fiat 1200 Spider, gutsy as they were, on the same track with a high-powered Ferrari or Cobra and expecting them to keep up.

Before Janet ever drove in a race, she attended yet another driving school. This one, sponsored by the SCCA, was held at Marlboro, Maryland.

There, in 1963, she learned all the things that every driver must know. How to get around the track in the midst of high-speed, howling traffic. How to accelerate on straightaways. How to pass. How to give way to faster drivers. How to shift through the corners. How to read the various flags that govern a race—flags such as green for the "course is clear," yellow for "danger," yellow with vertical red stripes for "oil on the track," and red for "pull over and stop because there's too much trouble up ahead."

Janet planned to begin racing in the XK-120, but she decided to buy a more powerful Jaguar, a used XK-140. Racing promised to be exciting—far more exciting than flying—but she knew it would be pretty frustrating, too. She realized that finely tuned cars can break down very easily after they've been run for hours at high speeds. They had to be fixed immediately if they were to get back onto the track or be ready for the next race you planned to enter. But it cost money to hire mechanics to do the fixing. It was money she couldn't really afford.

There was only one answer to the problem. She'd have to learn how to repair an engine herself.

But how to learn? Again, there was only one answer. Tear down an engine, study its every part, and then put it all back together again.

Oh boy! The job promised to be a back-breaking one. It would take months to complete. But it had to be done. And so a very determined Janet drove the XK-140 into an unused barn on Long Island. Out came the engine. It was set down in the back of an old station wagon.

Then, on arriving home from work every evening, Janet headed for the barn and rolled up her sleeves. Slowly, she took the engine apart and reassembled it. The job required all the patience she had. She used the Jaguar service manual as a guide, but said that it looked "like Greek" to her most of the time. The barn was without lights, forcing her to use a flashlight to see what she was doing. Worst of all, it was wintertime and the night air was biting cold. But, in three months, she was done. The XK-140, back together again, was ticking over smoothly, and Janet knew the workings of an automobile power plant as few people do.

She felt that she was now really prepared for competition. And compete she did. In 1963, her first year on the track, she drove in thirteen races. Then, in the next twelve years, she ran her total up to more than 120 races. She was behind the wheel at every opportunity, sometimes driving in local and regional events for the SCCA, sometimes in bigger events that got nationwide attention.

From the very start, Janet built a fine record for herself. Rarely do more than half the entries finish a sports car race, but Janet soon developed the habit of almost always being in there at the end. As often as not, she found herself finishing among the top ten cars.

Janet seemed especially good at endurance runs. These are long distance races that take hours to complete. One of her best early efforts saw her place sixth overall in a 500-miler at the Watkins Glen track. Another fine run was made in the six-hour race at Sebring in 1964. With her trusty XK-140, now eight years old but still a flashing blue, she placed second in class and fifth overall in the competition.

Then it was on to other tracks and other victories. In 1964 and 1965, she won two regional SCCA meets at the Bridgehampton track in New York, placed second in another, and third in still another. Those same years saw her racing in Connecticut, New Hampshire, Maryland, and Nassau in the Bahama Islands.

It was exhausting to work all week at the Republic Aviation plant and then dash off to race somewhere. But she loved every minute of it.

Back to Bridgehampton Janet went in 1966. There, she captured a second-in-class spot in the Can-Am Cup Races. She also took a second-in-class in the Watkins Glen 500. Then a third-in-class at the SCCA championship meet at Lime Rock, the very same spot where she had attended her first driving school.

Those first years were good and exciting ones for Janet. But the next ones were to be even better. Somewhere along the line, her ability had caught the attention of several people at the Macmillan Ring-Free Oil Company.

They had plans for her.

4

The Macmillan Motor Maids

The Macmillan company had long sponsored a team of men drivers in sports racing. But then, after watching the petite Smokey Drolet of Florida roar through the 1965 Bahama Speed Week, a top executive asked a question. There were some really fine women drivers around, and so why not also sponsor a women's team?

It wasn't just a good idea, the company thought. It was a great one. And how about this for a team name? The Macmillan Ring-Free Motor Maids.

Immediately, the search for the best women drivers was on. Smokey Drolet and Rosemary Smith were the first to join. Rosemary came from Ireland and had been named Europe's leading woman driver for 1965. Next, there were Suzy Dietrich of Ohio, Donna Mae Mims of Pennsylvania—famous for her love of the color pink—and Liane Engeman from Holland.

And, of course, Janet Guthrie.

Well known for her long distance successes, Janet was asked if she would like to join the Motor Maids for the 1966 endurance race at Daytona Beach, Florida. It was to run for a grueling twenty-four hours.

She accepted happily and then went on to race with the team until the early 1970s. For much of that time, Janet served as the Motor Maids' captain.

Janet not only raced for the team but also made many television appearances and gave public talks for the Macmillan company. On such occasions, she explained the work of the team and told of what it was like to race in a sports car.

Leonard F. Marino, who is now a vice-president for Macmillan, managed the team for many years. He recalls Janet as a highly intelligent woman who ranked among the most capable drivers in the United States. He says that she had a thorough knowledge of sports racing and that her leadership was greatly responsible for bringing the Motor Maids so many victories.

The team was a success right from the beginning. In the 1966 Daytona endurance classic, the Motor Maids fielded two cars. Janet, Suzy, and Donna Mae shared the driving chores in one. Smokey and Rosemary handled the other. Both groups stayed on the track for the entire twenty-four hours while other cars were dropping out all around. Janet and her co-drivers finished in twelfth place. Rosemary and Smokey came in eleventh.

Though Janet also continued to race on her own in the next years, she especially liked the Macmillan drives. When she raced by herself, she did so as an amateur, hoping to take home a trophy as a prize. The job of maintaining her car always kept her pocketbook stretched to the limit. But she was paid for her team drives, and that helped a lot. Also, the team drives gave her the experience of handling a number of different cars.

For instance, in the 1966 Daytona race, Janet and her co-drivers piloted a Sunbeam Alpine. Next, on returning to Daytona for the 1967 endurance run, Janet was assigned to a Mustang. Sharing the wheel with her were Smokey and a new Motor Maid, Anita Taylor. The three placed sixteenth and competed so well that they were awarded the KLG-Nosonger Trophy for the best performance by an all-girl team in the race.

That same year, Janet and Liane drove a Matra to a second-in-class in the Sebring twelve-hour enduro. Then came a second-in-class at Sebring in 1969, followed by a first-in-class in 1970. In the meantime, Janet had also handled such cars as Chevrons and Austin-Healeys.

The 1969 Sebring race earned the Motor Maids another KLG-Nosonger Trophy. Standing alongside their Austin-Healey Sprite, Janet, Liane, and Donna accepted the award and smilingly held it up for the news cameras.

All the Motor Maids were excellent drivers, and by 1970 they had set an enviable record. Not once had the team failed to finish a race.

But Janet herself held a record that was just as enviable. By 1971 she had run up a string of nine straight finishes in grueling endurance races. She now hoped that her tenth straight finish would come in the twelve-hour meet at Sebring. She and two teammates were scheduled to handle a B16 Chevron-Cotsworth FVC. At the last minute, however, they were shifted to a Chevron BMW.

The race was just one lap old when the Chevron BMW died. Janet pulled off the track, clear across the infield from the pits. Her job now was to get the car repaired on her own. Under the rules of the race, not one of her mechanics could touch the car for a mechanical problem without disqualifying it. Janet dashed across the infield to collect the tools needed for the job.

Armed with the tools—and with a mechanic who would serve as an adviser running close behind—Janet sprinted back to the car. Up snapped the hood and she went to work. It was work that lasted for an hour and a half. Several times, thinking that she had finally fixed things, she fired up the engine, only to hear it die in seconds. At last, she had to admit that it was no use. The car was definitely out of the race—and gone was her chance for a tenth straight endurance finish.

Janet was standing beside the track when the race ended. She had long worn a certain pair of driving gloves because she thought them lucky. They had been left behind in her original car when she was shifted to the Chevron BMW. Now she watched her car, with the lucky gloves somewhere inside, finish the race successfully. If only she had been behind the wheel . . .

She could only shrug off her disappointment with a smile. That was racing for you!

Other victories, however, soon made up for the disappointment. Sponsored by Macmillan and the Goodyear

Tire and Rubber Company, Janet drove a year-old Camaro to a first overall win in a three-hour endurance race at Bridgehampton in August 1971. Sharing the wheel with her in the 248-mile run was an ex-Marine named Kent Fellows.

Fellows drove for the first part of the race and built up a 26-second lead. But, when Janet took over, some precious time was lost because a tire was leaking and had to be changed. Another pit stop, this time for a mechanical adjustment, cut even deeper into the Camaro's lead. Then, topping things off, the brakes gave out. Fellows returned to the wheel for the final laps, and an admiring Janet said that he drove with "zero brakes." Still, the Camaro managed to hang on to its slim lead and was first to roar past the victory flag.

Janet was asked to join another racing team in 1971. This one was made up of Toyotas. Piloting a Celica, she captured the North Atlantic Road Racing championship in 1973. Two years later, at Bridgehampton, she took first place in both the Vanderbilt Cup run and the Bridgehampton 400. In the Vanderbilt race, she won out against twenty-seven men drivers.

By 1975, Janet Guthrie was one of the most respected drivers in sports car racing. She seemed to be getting better all the time, and she looked forward to many more exciting seasons on the track. But she had no idea that the most exciting season of all lay just ahead and that once again her life was about to change overnight.

This time, the change started with a surprising telephone call.

5

First Step to Indy

When Janet answered the phone, there was a man named Rolla Vollstedt at the other end of the line. Gray-haired and sharp-featured, he was an Oregon lumber executive whose great love in life was auto racing. He had been building his own championship cars for years now. They had competed in the Indianapolis 500 since 1962.

Vollstedt had a question for Janet. He was planning to enter two cars in the 1976 Indianapolis race. One was to be handled by his long-time driver, Dick Simon. Vollstedt wanted to have a woman at the wheel of the second car. Would Janet like to try for the job?

The question was so unexpected that it left Janet speechless. She had often thought about driving in Indy-type races. But championship-car racing was strictly a man's world, and friends had told her to forget it. Women just didn't have the strength and skill to handle those turbocharged rockets. This was nonsense, she knew. Today's women were making great advances on all job fronts, doing many things that no one had ever thought they'd be able to do. So why shouldn't a woman compete in the big cars?

But old ideas are hard to break down, and so she had always put thoughts of championship-car racing out of her mind.

And now, suddenly, she was being given the chance of a lifetime. Vollstedt wasn't just asking her to try out for one of the many Indy-type races that are held each year across the country. He was asking her to try for the granddaddy of them all—the Indianapolis 500 itself.

Janet heard him say that he wanted to be the first car owner to send a woman to the race. He felt that women deserved the chance. But he openly admitted that a woman driver would also give his car much publicity.

Then Janet found her voice. Yes, she said quickly, she'd be happy to drive for Vollstedt. She later told reporters that she answered quickly so that he wouldn't have the chance to change his mind.

She asked him how he had come to pick her. The answer was simple. When Vollstedt had started to look for a woman driver, he had gone to the SCCA for advice. The club kept a list of 6,000 drivers. Of that number, 100 were women. The SCCA officials said that the top woman on the list was Janet Guthrie.

Vollstedt had nodded and hurried to a telephone.

Once Janet had said her quick "yes," Vollstedt got down to a problem that had to be faced. He knew she was a fine sports car driver—the best. He wanted her in his car. But, let's face it, Indy racers are three times as powerful as sports cars. Before Janet could hope to enter the 500, she would have to prove that she could actually handle a championship car. The proof was to be had in two steps.

First, Vollstedt wanted her to come to the Ontario Speedway in the Los Angeles area. There, she would climb into one of his cars and run a series of speed tests under the watchful eye of his number-one driver, Dick Simon. If she passed the tests, she would take the second step and compete in the Trenton 200. Held in New Jersey a month before the 500, it would show whether she had what it took to handle a championship car under actual racing conditions.

Vollstedt then reminded her that all big-car races are supervised by the United States Auto Club (USAC). He said he was sure that if Janet performed well at Trenton, the USAC and the officials at Indianapolis would be happy to let her try for a spot in the 500. But if she didn't . . .

Janet knew the answer to that.

A week in February 1976 was set for the Ontario tests. They were to be held in complete secrecy. Vollstedt didn't want the news of his Indy plans to slip out until Janet had passed the tests and was ready for the Trenton 200. Then he would hit the sports pages with the biggest racing story in years—perhaps the biggest of the century.

Janet looked forward to the speed tests with mixed

31

feelings. On the one hand, she was excited about getting into her first championship car. And she was thrilled at the thought of going to Indianapolis. The venerable old track, with its 2.5-mile racing oval, had been the goal of drivers everywhere since 1911, when the first 500 was held. Through the years since, the cars had gotten more and more powerful and the race had seen some fantastic speeds, speeds that steadily mounted from 74.59 mph in 1911 to more than 175 mph in 1975. And through the years the 500 had grown in popularity until it now attracted more than a million spectators each Memorial Day Weekend.

But, on the other hand, Janet felt uneasy. She knew that she was headed for trouble. She was going to be breaking into a man's world. A great storm was sure to burst over her head. Countless people would want her to succeed. Countless others would be against her, and they'd say that she was just a "women's libber" who was butting into a world where she had no place. It wasn't going to be fun to hear such things and see them printed on the sports pages.

She didn't know it, but the trouble had already started. Dick Simon was dead against Vollstedt's plan. He thought it was all meant to grab newspaper space. When agreeing to supervise the speed tests, he said that Janet had better be darned good if she hoped to pass. Indy driving was rugged and the competition the best. She'd really have to prove herself to him. No way was he going to be "a baby-sitter for a publicity stunt."

As the date for the tests approached, Janet's excitement grew. She could hardly wait. But then, during a visit to San Francisco just ten days before she was due at Ontario, a freak accident almost ruined her chances. It happened while she was doing some conditioning exercises.

One was a jumping exercise, and somehow she landed the wrong way. There was a sudden pain in her left foot. Then redness and swelling. A visit to a doctor ended with bad news. A bone was broken.

Over Janet's protests, the doctor put the foot in a cast. She hobbled out on crutches and wondered how on earth she was ever going to get an Indy car around the track with a plaster-of-Paris "shoe" clear up past her ankle. But she was determined to make the tests. Nothing was going to stop her. There was just one thing to do. Hunt up a doctor who would remove the cast.

But no such doctor could be found. All said it would be too dangerous. Then Mary McGee, a good friend and fellow sports car driver, came to the rescue. She showed Janet how the cast could be soaked in water until it was soft enough to be broken.

And so, when Janet stepped off the airliner at Ontario, she was limping—but the cast and crutches were gone. Instead, her foot was tightly wrapped in Ace bandages. Vollstedt saw the limp and his eyebrows went up. As casually as she could, Janet explained that she had sprained the foot while out for a walk. It was nothing. Really.

She sighed with relief when Vollstedt said nothing, but simply drove her to the track. Some days later, she told him the truth. He grinned as if he'd known all along and said she wasn't the first driver to pretend that something didn't hurt. He recalled that Simon had once driven in a race with third-degree burns on his leg. Running well, Dick had refused to stop until crossing the finish line. Then he had passed out with the pain.

Simon was waiting at the track. He was ready to be a hard taskmaster, but no sooner had he met Janet than he began to like this young woman. She listened attentively when he introduced her to the car and explained its workings. She asked sensible questions. Soon, the two of them were talking together as driver to driver. Maybe, he thought, Janet Guthrie wasn't going to need a baby-sitter after all.

Then, once out on the track, she won him over even more. Though new to the turbocharged car, she drove smoothly and expertly. On her first day, she roared up to 160 mph. Within a few more days, she was hitting 172.58 mph, a speed that everyone felt would be needed to qualify for the 500. And, on the straightaways, Simon clocked her at 196 mph. Yes, indeed, this girl was turning out fine.

As for Janet, the experience was a thrilling one. She had never handled so much power in her whole life. And she would never forget her feelings the first time she brought the racer up to speed and the turbocharger ignited. The car seemed to shoot right out from beneath her. As she was to say often from then on, it had been like "going to the moon."

There was one problem, however. As a sports driver,

34

The 500 rolls at Indy. (Photo courtesy Indianapolis Motor Speedway Corporation)

Gasoline Alley at Indianapolis. It was completely a man's world—until Janet arrived. (Photo courtesy Indianapolis Motor Speedway Corporation)

*An excited and determined
Janet soon after
her arrival
in Indianapolis.
(Photo courtesy
Indianapolis Motor
Speedway Corporation)*

*Fast action in the pits
at Indianapolis.
(Photo courtesy
Indianapolis Motor
Speedway Corporation)*

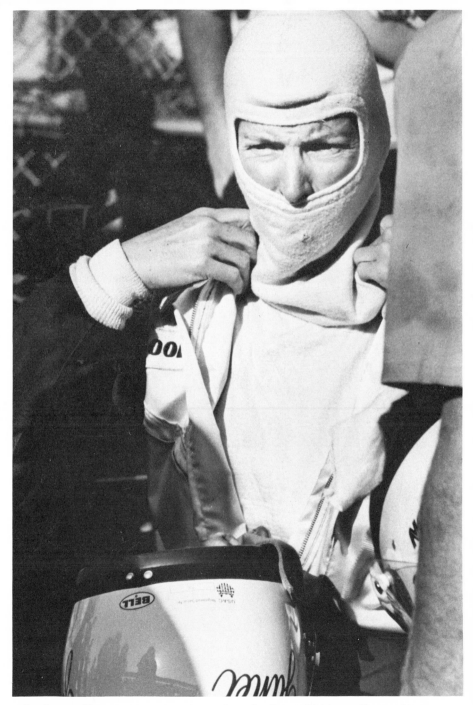

Ready to go! Her expression serious, Janet adjusts her fireproof driving uniform as she prepares to become the first woman to drive a practice run for the Indianapolis 500. (United Press International Photo)

It's a "thumbs up" signal from Rolla Vollstedt, the Bryant Special's *owner, as Janet heads for the Indy track and a practice run.* (United Press Intrernational Photo)

As the first woman ever to try for the 500, Janet was always the center of much attention at Indianapolis. Here, fans and news cameramen stand by as she moves onto the track for a practice run. (United Press International Photo)

All the attention given to Janet continued even when she wasn't in the Special. *Wherever she went, there were newsmen with questions—and fans with programs and autograph books to be signed. This picture catches her as she greets some young admirers with the wide Guthrie smile.* (United Press International Photo)

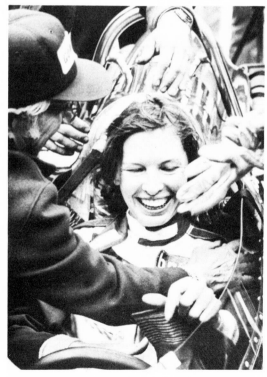

Though she had to be towed from the track when the Bryant Special *broke down after just a few laps, Janet still pulled off her face mask with a happy smile.*
She had just become the first woman to run through practice laps for the 500. United Press International Photo)

Another smile from Janet—this time as she returned to the pits after successfully completing her rookie tests for the 500.
Reaching in to pat her on the shoulder is Rolla Vollstedt. (United Press International Photo)

Janet had never before worked on an oval track used by championship cars. She was not used to the concrete wall that circles the outside edge of the track. Looming constantly on the right, it can be a pretty terrifying blur at speeds of over 100 mph. Janet stayed well clear of the thing and the disaster it promised.

This was a mistake and Simon pointed it out to her. To hold the best speed possible, he explained, a car should zoom right up close to the wall when coming out of a turn. On a sheet of paper, he sketched a diagram of the track and showed her the path that must be taken. He didn't seem to be disappointed in her because, as he said, the wall never fails to frighten a rookie driver. But *she* was angry—furious with herself for having let fear cause such an error.

While Simon prepped the racer for its next run, Janet walked over to Rolla Vollstedt and borrowed the passenger car he had rented for trips to and from the track. Quietly, she attached a four-inch welding bar into the right-hand door. Then, with the rod jutting straight out from the door, she circled the track time and again. On each turn, she came a little closer to the wall. It rushed by in a gray, threatening haze. Suddenly, she heard metal scraping against concrete. Good! She wasn't satisfied until she could hear that screeching noise above the engine roar on every turn. At last, she returned to the pits, got out from behind the wheel, and went around to look at the bar.

It was worn completely away. Even some of the paint on the door was gone.

Well, she thought, that's more like it!

A few minutes later, Janet was in the racer. Dick Simon and Rolla Vollstedt watched her zoom through the run. The wall was no problem now. Simon said she came so close to it that she scared the life out of Vollstedt. As for Simon himself, he later told reporters that "I knew right then this girl could make it at Indy."

At the end of the speed tests, Janet climbed out of the car to be greeted by a smiling Simon and Vollstedt. There were handshakes and congratulations all around. She had proved herself more than capable of handling a championship car—even with a broken bone in her foot.

Now it was time to announce the big Indy plan and get on with the second step—the Trenton 200.

6

Hard Words

The big plan was announced in early March. Startled reporters heard that, for the first time in racing history, a woman was going to try for the 500. But first she would go to the Trenton 200. Suddenly, the name of Janet Guthrie popped up on sports pages everywhere, along with the name of her car, the *Bryant Special,* so christened because it was sponsored by the Bryant Heating and Air Conditioning Company.

Almost overnight, the storm of argument that Janet had expected broke out over her head. There were people throughout the country who thought she was doing something great and wished her luck. But there were others who had nothing but criticism for her. They said all the usual things—that no woman had the strength or the skill for the race. Just who did she think she was?

The harshest criticism came from the men who were planning to drive at Indy. They had all put in time on what is known as the "Championship Trail." The "Trail" is made up of grueling big-car races that are held around the country each year. It's a rugged, uphill climb that leads finally to the greatest race of all—the 500. These men were tough, proud, capable. They felt that, by learning their business the hard way, they had won the right to compete at Indy. Now here was this woman saying that she was going to start right at the top.

One of the most outspoken critics turned out to be the quiet Bobby Unser, who had taken Indy wins in 1968 and 1975—the previous year. He said nothing against Janet's abilities as a sports car driver and explained that he wasn't opposed to women racing in championship cars. It's just that they should earn the right to do so, he said. He dubbed Janet's entry as a publicity stunt that could be blamed on the "women's lib" movement.

Johnny Rutherford, whose speed of 158.589 mph had won him the 1974 Indy race, agreed with Unser. He didn't think there were any women drivers, no matter how good, who had the experience necessary for Indy competition.

Bill Vukovich, the Indy winner in 1953 and 1954, said bluntly that he'd eat his hat if Janet—or any other woman—performed well in a championship car. One day, while watching her make a practice run for the Trenton race, Vukovich grinned and said she looked nice. Nice and slow!

Lurking behind all the criticism was a strong sense of worry—the worry that Janet would be a danger to everyone on the track. The men had reason to be concerned. They were remembering the Arlene Hiss case.

Though Janet was the first woman to try for the 500, she was not the first to compete in a big-car race. Arlene Hiss, a dancing teacher and the former wife of driver Mike Hiss, had taken that honor by competing in the Phoenix 150 at about the time of Janet's Indy announcement. Arlene had posted some fine speeds in practice runs, but she had been "black flagged" in the race itself for driving too slowly. She had placed last and had heard seven drivers say angrily that her slowness had been a terrible danger to the cars roaring past.

Now would the same thing happen to Janet? That was the big question—the big fear—in the men's minds.

If Janet was hurt or angered by what was being said, she did not show it. Reporters swarmed around her constantly now. They all had questions that were based on the criticisms. She never failed to give quiet, thoughtful answers.

"Do you really think you have the physical strength to handle an Indy car?"

Janet said she thought so. She pointed out that there were no "skeletal differences" that would make a man better able to handle the car. Perhaps a man could outdo a woman in golf or tennis by hitting the ball harder and farther. But, in racing, physical strength by itself didn't count all that much. More important were skill, co-ordination, courage, and the ability to concentrate. These were qualities that women had just as much as men.

"What about the Indy competition? Can you stand up to it?"

Janet answered by saying that in sports car racing she had competed successfully against Mark Donohue, Dan Gurney, and Peter Revson. They all had international reputations and were among the best men drivers in racing.

"Do you think you'll be a danger to the other drivers?"

Janet shook her head. She was going to drive carefully. But she also planned to drive competitively, at the best speed she could attain. All the while, she would concentrate on not getting in the way of faster cars. If she had anything to do about it, she'd be a danger to no one.

"Do you really think you're good enough for Indy?"

She replied that, in her own mind, she thought she was a good driver. She didn't know if she was another Mark Donohue. But at last she was getting the chance to find out just how good she really was. She was going to give it her best shot.

The Trenton 200—or Trentonian, as it is also called—was scheduled for Sunday, April 25, 1976. Janet arrived at the 1.5-mile oval track at mid-month to begin her practice sessions. From the start, she gave the other drivers little to complain about. Her first practice run saw her accelerate the *Bryant Special* up to 145 mph. In the next days, she moved past 150 mph, and then past the 155 mark.

Though not the best speeds in the world—and far behind the 165.2 clocked by Johnny Rutherford—they weren't bad, especially when everyone knew that she was concentrating on learning the track and finding the "groove"—that shortest path around the course. Slowly, Janet began to earn the respect of such drivers as Tom Sneva. When the Indy veteran met her one morning, Janet asked him a number of questions about the condition of the track and its rough spots. Sneva said he could tell right away that she was a calm and experienced driver, even if brand new to championship cars.

But, as calm as she appeared to be, Janet couldn't help but be nervous on the inside. Wherever she looked, she saw the fans who had come out to view the practice sessions; they were all watching her closely. And wherever she looked, she saw some of the world's best and most experienced drivers. Bobby Unser, Bill Vukovich, and Johnny Rutherford, all of whom were so opposed to her being here. Gordon Johncock. And the great A. J. Foyt. This year, he was trying to do what no other driver had ever done—win the Indy 500 for the fourth time.

Janet knew that, no matter how well she was doing in practice, everyone was waiting for her to make a mistake. A mistake was something she just couldn't afford. In the race, it could prove disastrous. And in practice, it could make her look foolish and might cause the USAC and the people at Indy to turn down her application for the 500. Wouldn't that please everyone who said a woman had no place in a championship car?

To make matters worse, she had two hurdles yet to

clear before she even got into the Trentonian. First, she had to run some practice laps while USAC officials watched. The Club had granted her permission to try for the Trentonian, but it had been only temporary permission. Before final permission was given, she had to show the officials that she was good enough for the race.

Second, once that final permission was obtained, Janet had to qualify for the race. Twenty-six cars were on hand for the Trentonian. But only the fastest twenty-two would be on the track when the starter's flag came down. The *Bryant Special* just had to be one of them!

Janet needn't have worried about either problem. On the weekend of the race, she won final USAC permission by driving smoothly at a speed of more than 150 mph. Then, when the time came for the qualifying laps, she gunned the *Special* up to 156.886 mph. Other drivers put in qualifying speeds in excess of 160 mph, but Janet's run was good enough to earn her the fourteenth starting position in the twenty-two-car field.

Now came the toughest hurdle of all—the one that really put butterflies in her stomach. The race itself!

Janet went out to a restaurant with Rolla Vollstedt, Dick Simon, and the *Special's* crew on the night before the Trentonian. During dinner, as a token of their admiration, the Vollstedt team gave her a small cake decorated with two sparklers. A very touched Janet returned home to her trailer in the Trenton infield for some restful sleep. Come what may, she was ready for tomorrow.

But she awoke to bad news. It was raining and there was talk of postponing the Trentonian. At midday, the final decision came through. The race was off until Sunday, May 2.

Janet would have to put up with those butterflies for another week.

7

The Trentonian

The butterflies stayed with Janet all through the long week. They seemed to have doubled in number by Sunday, May 2.

But what else could she expect? The Trentonian was to be one of the most important races in her career. Not only would it mark her first time out in traffic in a championship car, but it still loomed as the last big hurdle on the road to Indy. So far, in her practice and qualifying sessions, she had done well and the USAC seemed more and more willing to let her try for the 500. Now if she could do a really good job today . . .

Everyone who encountered Janet on the morning of the race could see the tension inside her. Reporter Michael Katz of the New York *Times* wrote that she was as nervous as a high school student waiting to take a college-entrance exam. Jackie Stewart, the former world's driving champion who was now covering motor sports for ABC television, came upon Janet while she was sitting in the *Special* before a practice run. Stewart said he had one sure way of knowing that a driver was nervous. He just looked at the visor on the crash helmet to see if it was steaming with body heat. Well, that's exactly what this newcomer's visor was doing.

Nervousness was not all that Janet felt, however. Mingled with it was a deep sense of pleasure. She saw that the other drivers seemed no longer troubled by her presence, a sure indication that she was winning their respect. Several came up to her and, grinning, asked her to autograph their programs. Then A. J. Foyt approached, welcomed her to the world of big-car racing, and wished her luck. After he had departed, Janet had just one thing to say about Foyt: he was great—truly a "big guy."

And Janet couldn't help but be pleased by something Bobby Unser said. His *Eagle* had broken its front suspension during the morning practice sessions and he was due to watch the race from the sidelines. He told reporters that he would certainly apologize for his earlier remarks if Janet went on to qualify for the 500.

The Trentonian was scheduled to roll at 1:45 P.M. By 1:30, the cars were stationed in the grid and ready to go. More than 16,000 people jammed the grandstands. Cheers rolled across the track when George Hamid, Jr., the promoter of the race, picked up the public address microphone and introduced each driver.

Janet and A. J. Foyt were called to the microphone, Foyt because he had qualified fastest with a clocking of 166.307 mph, and Janet because she was making racing history today. Hamid called Janet a "lovely bundle of courage" and she told the fans how happy she was to be in the Trentonian and that she'd do her best to give them their money's worth. Then she was back in the *Special* and lowering that "steaming" visor into place.

For years, the Trentonian and other championship-car races had always begun with the words, "Gentlemen, start your engines." But today, the announcement was to be different and a sign of how things were changing in racing. Today, Hamid placed the public address microphone close to his mouth and shouted:

"Janet and gentlemen, start your engines!"

Later, Janet was to remark that she wished Hamid had simply said, "Championship drivers, start your engines." She still wanted to be accepted not as a woman driver but as a driver, period. But, once she heard the words, she had no time to think of her feelings. The thunderous roar of engines filled the afternoon air.

In the next instant, the racers were moving. With the pace car leading, they circled the one-and-a-half-mile oval twice to warm the engines. Then the pace car angled off the track. The starter whipped his flag up and down. The Trentonian was on.

Watching from the pit, Vollstedt and his crew were delighted with Janet's performance. She wasn't acting as if this was her first big-car race. She was streaking along and staying right in there with everyone else—which was more than could be said of two more experienced drivers. Hardly had the race started before Bill Vukovich's car broke a valve and dropped out for good.

Then, minutes later, A. J. Foyt ended his day with a blown engine.

Over on the sidelines, Vukovich was remembering what he'd said about eating his hat if any woman did well in a championship car. Well, here he was, out of the competition. And there Janet was, still on the track. Vukovich had been the first to drop out and so would be ranked in bottom place when the final standings for the race were listed. No matter what happened to Janet or her car, she would place higher than he—and A. J. Foyt. Vukovich smiled and admitted to reporters that Janet was looking "definitely more qualified" for championship-car racing than he had first thought.

There were congratulations and pats on the back when Janet came in for her first pit stop. It was a routine one for refueling. She took a few swallows of Gatorade as the crew quickly went over the car. Then the *Special* was moving and heading back out into traffic.

But, moments later, a crewman waved frantically to his fellow mechanics. He was wearing a headset that was connected to a microphone on Janet's helmet. He began to shout that she was saying something about returning to the pits. He didn't know why. He couldn't hear her clearly. But she was coming in!

The men stared at each other. What had gone wrong?

It was a frustrated Janet who braked to a stop alongside them. Her helmet was giving her trouble because the chinstrap had somehow loosened during the previous pit stop. Those few swallows of Gatorade had been just enough to disturb the buckle. Janet later called it "a dumb thing" that had never happened before. But now she sat impatiently while a mechanic tried to tighten the strap. It refused to stay put. Janet finally waved him away. Too much precious time was being lost. She'd have to live with the darned thing. The *Special's* engine roared and she was gone.

Despite the problem, Janet continued to drive smoothly. Up against such competition as front runners Gordon Johncock, Johnny Rutherford, and Tom Sneva, she was far back in the pack and had little or no chance of winning. But Vollstedt and his team had never expected her to win. After all, this *was* her first big-car race. All they wanted her to do was drive expertly so that the USAC would have no reason to keep her from going to Indy.

Swiftly, the laps rolled out from beneath the cars. Janet pulled into the pits once more, this time to change a tire that had been cut. She was gone again in a flash and back into the groove and looking good—very good indeed!

If she could just keep it up . . . .

But, suddenly, there was trouble. It came unexpectedly just after the seventieth lap.

As she was heading through the curve, Janet saw a faster car roaring up to pass. She tried to give the driver room. But, in doing so, she pulled the *Special* far down to her left. The wheels caught the "marbles"—the sand that bordered the low side of the track. Instantly, Janet felt the car skid and begin to spin.

The crowd of 16,000 gasped as Janet fought to keep

from turning sideways to the oncoming traffic. Cars zoomed by in a blur. There! She was straightening out. But what was that? She heard the engine cut out.

Desperately, Janet worked the gearshift and clutch. The engine fired again. Bless it! Then, as suddenly as the trouble had started, it was over. The *Special* was aimed in the right direction and gathering speed. Up in the stands, the gasp turned into a giant sigh of relief.

But there were no sighs of relief from Janet as she drove through the next laps. She had gotten out of the skid and avoided disaster only to find herself in deeper trouble. When straightening and restarting the car, she had put too much strain on the gearbox. Much too much, from the sound of things. Something had broken loose inside. She could hear it rattling around and punching holes in the transmission.

She shook her head. With the transmission damaged, she didn't dare go on for fear of harming the car even more. She had now completed seventy-nine laps and the *Special* was finished for the day. A disappointed Janet came down the straightaway in front of the grandstand for the last time and headed into the pits.

Janet climbed out of the *Special* to hear someone ask her how she felt. She had a single-word reply:

"Frustrated."

The frustration did not last for long, however. Janet learned that, at the time the *Special* dropped out, she had been running eleventh among the fourteen cars left in the race. She was going to be placed fifteenth in the Trentonian's rankings—three notches above the great A.J.

and seven above last-place Bill Vukovich. She told reporters she was sure she would have finished in the top ten had she been able to continue. But she couldn't help but be happy with the fifteenth spot. For a newcomer to big-car racing, she had made a good showing, one that gave the USAC no cause for complaint.

Janet stood in the pits and watched the Trentonian end in an astonishing way. Gordon Johncock, who had won the Indy 500 in 1973, took the lead on lap 107 and held it until the next-to-last lap. Then, with Johnny Rutherford running just five seconds behind, Johncock's engine died without warning. He headed into the pits and groaned when the problem turned out to be a simple one that can nevertheless give any driver nightmares. With just a scant distance to go—and with victory in his grasp—he had run smack out of fuel.

While his crew splashed in just enough to get him started again, Johncock sat there and watched Rutherford flash by. Seconds later, Rutherford was streaking across the finish line under the victory flag.

But Johncock wasn't done yet. He shot back out onto the track and held off a fast-closing Tom Sneva to take second place.

When interviewed after the race, Rutherford said that he had been dumbfounded to see Johncock's car lose speed. He had thought the cars were being slowed by the yellow flag because there was trouble up ahead. But then, on looking around, he had seen no yellow flag. Rutherford grinned and finished off by saying that he had been in just "the right place at the right time."

Rutherford's words came as he stood before a microphone in the track press room. The place was crowded with reporters, drivers, mechanics, car owners, and fans. Janet could be seen near the door. Suddenly, she heard her name being mentioned. A reporter wanted to know if Rutherford thought she had driven well.

The reply was straight to the point. Rutherford could find no fault with Janet's performance. She had driven well in her first big-car race and was bound to do better the next time. Rutherford—whom Janet later called a "real gentleman"—wished her luck in the coming 500.

And so one of the biggest days in Janet Guthrie's life ended. She had done a good job. She had shown the USAC that she was capable of driving at Indy. And she had won the respect of the men who had doubted her abilities.

There was just one thing left for her to do:

Head for the 500.

8

Arrival at Indy

Janet arrived at the Indianapolis Speedway on Saturday, May 8. Eager to begin the three weeks of practice needed for the 500, she looked at the grandstands sweeping along the main straightaway. She gazed up at the tower that flashed the positions of the cars in a race. She walked through Gasoline Alley, the garage area where the racers were prepped before being taken out on the track. Imagine the emotions that swept through her.

First, there was excitement. At long last, here she was at the greatest championship track in the country. Everywhere, there was the feel of history. The world's most powerful cars had battled it out here through the years since the first 500 in 1911. The world's best drivers had zoomed along that straightaway and had relaxed here in Gasoline Alley. Some had driven to glory. Some to defeat. And some to death.

There was even history in the track's nickname—the

"Brickyard." Someone long ago had coined the name because the 2.5-mile oval had been originally paved with bricks. The bricks, now covered over with concrete, were no longer visible. But the nickname still remained and had become a part of racing lore.

Yes. There was history everywhere. And now she was going to be a part of it.

Along with her excitement, there was a sense of relief. Though knowing she had done well in the Trentonian, Janet had still put in a long day of waiting before word came through that she had been cleared for the 500 try. Actually, she had only been cleared to take the "rookie test" that is demanded of all drivers new to Indy. It would call for her to lap the track at specified speeds on two different occasions. Once she passed the test, she could go ahead and try to qualify for a spot in the 500.

Finally, Janet was nervous. This was a place of racing history, and she knew she was going to make history of her own in the next days. If all went well, she was going to become:

The first woman to drive a practice run at Indy.

The first woman to take the 500's rookie test.

The first woman to qualify for the 500.

And—hope of hopes—the first woman ever to compete in the race.

The pressure was back on again. People everywhere were going to be watching her. Some would be pulling for her. Some would be waiting for her to make a mistake. It would be the Trentonian all over again. Only this time the pressure was greater because at stake was the 500.

Not helping Janet's nervousness at all was the airline that brought her to Indianapolis. Somehow, the baggage crew had lost her suitcases. Her driving suit, helmet, and gloves were nowhere to be seen and would remain in hiding for a day or so. In the meantime, Bill Vukovich came to Janet's rescue and loaned her a complete driving outfit. Vukovich hadn't "eaten his hat" yet, but he willingly gave her a helmet to wear.

Far more nerve wracking than the lost luggage was the fact that the *Bryant Special* had begun to act up. Janet planned to make her first practice run on the day of her arrival, but a bad clutch hub kept the mechanics working on the car until late in the afternoon. Then Dick Simon got behind the wheel for several laps of testing, only to have an oil line break.

Things were no better on Sunday. Again, Simon tested the *Special*, wanting now to double check the suspension system before turning the car over to Janet. He made it around the track just twice before he drew into the pits with a grim look. A piston had burned out.

Janet could only groan. At this rate, she might never get the chance to become the first woman to practice at Indy.

Her chance, however, did come on Monday. She made her bit of history, but could only feel discouraged about the whole thing. Though she started out smoothly enough, she had to pull into the pits with a troubled wheel bearing at the end of two laps. A change was quickly made, though, and Janet was soon running again.

But this time, she lasted only four laps, just long enough to get the tires warmed up. Then, as she put it, she felt the engine "go soft." She shut the Offenhauser down on the main straightaway and angled off the track some distance from the pits.

She sat quietly for a few moments until a truck arrived. A tow line was tossed to her. She held it firmly while the *Special* was towed back to the pits. The problem: another burned piston. No, not another one, but the same one that had gone out on Simon. It had caused a fitting in the fuel delivery line to crack.

Some historic moment! A mere six laps and a damaged engine!

Now Janet could only hope that the *Special* would behave during her rookie test, which was scheduled for Tuesday, May 11. In the morning, she was to lap the track twenty times—a distance of fifty miles—at 160 mph. The afternoon would see her do another twenty laps, this time at 165 mph.

Watching the whole time would be four experienced Indy drivers. They were Gary Bettenhausen, Al Loquasto, Jr., Tom Bigelow, and Graham McCrae. They would decide whether she passed or failed the test.

The sky was overcast on Tuesday morning when Janet headed along the main straightaway at the start of her first run. Her eyes flicked back and forth between the gauges and the track. The *Special* responded nicely as she increased her speed, warming the car up before accelerating to the necessary 160 mph. Now if it would only go on behaving . . .

It did. But just for six laps, a distance of about fifteen miles. Then the oil pressure gauge registered a sudden drop. Face tense, Janet drove into the pits. She climbed out of the car and, for the first time, let all the tension and frustration within her be seen. The driver who had always been so calm during the long days at Trenton now tore off her gloves angrily and paced up and down beside the car.

More than 50,000 fans waited—for fifteen minutes while the Vollstedt crew repaired the *Special*. Then they saw Janet climb back into the cockpit and tug her helmet into place. A cheer that echoed across the infield welcomed her return to the track.

Now—miracle of miracles—the *Special* decided to cooperate. The Offenhauser engine roared smoothly as Janet circled the track again and again, finding the groove and no longer shying away from the concrete wall as she had first done at Ontario. She was a triumphant young woman when the twentieth lap rolled out from under the car and she braked to a stop. The final verdict would come from Bettenhausen and his fellow drivers, but Janet was certain she had passed the first part of the test. She had run at the required 160 mph and had driven well.

Now she had some time to relax before the second phase of the test. It was a wait that was marked by a spectacular crash involving another rookie, Eddie Miller of Lakewood, Colorado. As he was streaking through a practice curve at 167 mph, Miller veered wide and came within inches of hitting the concrete wall. He threw the wheel over to save himself, with the result that his car went into a skid that sent it slithering across the track. The out-of-control racer hurtled into the infield and headed for an area crowded with spectators.

Before it reached them, however, the car flew across a drainage ditch and buried its nose in the far bank. The racer catapulted into the air, cleared a five-foot fence, and came down with a rending crash between a telephone pole and a tree. Somehow, neither was touched.

But the crash didn't end there. On hitting the ground, the car bounced high again. Now, twisting and turning, it sailed over an eight-foot-high fence and into the spectator area. Screaming, people fled in all directions to avoid the plummeting wreckage. Miraculously, the car struck no one. It smashed into the ground and bounced up against another fence, at last coming to rest there.

Track workers and medical attendants rushed to Miller's aid. They found him still alive and still conscious in the crushed metal. He was worked free with crowbars and rushed by ambulance to Methodist Hospital in Indianapolis. There, doctors called him one of the luckiest men around. His most serious injury: two broken vertebrae in the neck.

The crash delayed the practice activities scheduled for the remainder of the day and time ran out before Janet could continue her test. She was thwarted the next day when the *Special* decided to be temperamental again. It

But now it's a thoughtful expression as the crew works on the troubled Special. *In addition to its mechanical problems, the car could not reach the speed of 181mph, which was needed to put it in the range for qualifying for the 500.* (United Press International Photo)

Despite all the problems with the Special, this is one of the few times that the camera caught Janet with a grim expression. She describes a problem of handling her car to Indy veteran Johnny Rutherford. Rutherford went on the win in the 1976 running of the 500. (United Press International Photo)

A thoughtful Janet and her crew talk over her practice laps for NASCAR's World 600. The man at the right of the picture is crew chief, Ralph Moody. (United Press International Photo)

Before going out to qualify for the 600, Janet talked about track conditions with veteran NASCAR driver Donnie Allison. Allison also had some tips for her on how to handle a stock car. Later, Janet said that Allison's advice had helped her greatly in reaching a qualifying speed. (United Press International Photo)

A very pleased Janet climbs out of her car after a good practice run for the World 600. A short time later, she qualified for the race with a speed of 152.797 mph. (United Press International Photo)

Now it's a triumphant Janet as the camera catches her at the end of the World 600. She placed fifteenth in the race—a great showing for a rookie stock car driver. The 600 is the longest event on the NASCAR circuit. (United Press International Photo)

It's not all driving. Janet helps her crew push her car into position for a practice run at Daytona. After the 600, Janet went on the place fifteenth in the Firecracker 400 at Daytona. Then she placed twelfth in the Richmond 400—the highest spot taken by a rookie that day. (United Press International Photo)

Janet Guthrie—ready for more NASCAR races and ready for another try at Indianapolis.
(United Press International Photo)

came up with an ignition problem when Dick Simon went out for a test run. For five hours, the problem resisted every effort to correct it.

In the meantime, Janet stood by and watched the other drivers take their practice runs. Some fantastic speeds went into the books. Johnny Rutherford fired his McLaren up to 188.363 mph one day and then followed it next day with 183.748. A. J. Foyt reached 187.839, Bobby Unser got to 187.343, and Tom Sneva came in with 185.109. Then there was Mario Andretti with 184.843, and Gordon Johncock with 182.

These weren't just fantastic speeds. They were also speeds that worried Janet and the Vollstedt crew. It was becoming clearer by the day that a car would have to hit at least 180 mph to qualify for the 500. Could the *Special*, beset by one mechanical problem after another since its arrival, possibly reach that speed without falling apart?

Janet saw the mechanics shake their heads with doubt.

After a further delay caused by rain, Janet was able to take the second part of her rookie test on May 17. Hoping that all would be well with the *Special*, she worked her way steadily up to the 165 mark. She held to the groove while the concrete wall and the grandstands beyond shot past in a grayish blur. On one lap, she reached 174.429 mph. She learned later that her time just missed tying the closed-course record held by a woman. Paula Murphy, driving a Dodge stock car, was the record holder.

But Janet wasn't thinking of records as she came

through the final laps. All she wanted was to have the *Special* hang together long enough for her to finish. All she wanted was to get through the rest of a test without some mistake . . .

And then it was over and she was back in the pits. Vollstedt, Dick Simon, and the crew were swarming about her with congratulations. Flashbulbs popped as the news photographers arrived. Reporters threw questions at her and added their own congratulations. Everyone was sure that she'd passed the test with flying colors.

Janet felt they were right, but she had to make certain. She hurried over to the office where Bettenhausen and the other driver judges were waiting. She opened the door—and felt her heart skip a beat.

The four men stared at her out of serious, troubled eyes. They shook their heads. Then, seeming to hate every word, they started to accuse her of "being afraid" of the wall and shying away from it. Of being shaky at the wheel. Of driving erratically. Janet stood there, dumbfounded.

It was the worst news possible.

And, considering how everyone down in the pits felt, it made no sense at all.

But, suddenly, the men couldn't keep up the pretense any longer. Grins—and then laughter—broke out all over the room. And, with the joke over, the words did a complete about-face. She'd done beautifully. Stayed right in the groove. Hit the necessary speed. And handled the wheel like an expert. And she'd been cleared for a try at the qualification runs.

It was the very news that Janet had been waiting to hear.

Now if only the *Special* would do its part.

9

The Coyote Incident

Unfortunately, the *Special* refused "to do its part" in the next days of practice. Try as she might, Janet could only nurse the car up to around 171 mph. Vollstedt went so far as to have the engine replaced four times, but to no avail. Somehow, the racer just couldn't find the power to reach the 180 mark that would be needed for qualification.

And there were continuing mechanical problems. Burned pistons remained at the head of the list. One morning, the car broke down far out on the track and had to be towed in. On another occasion, while Dick Simon was making a test run, something on the track flew into the turbocharger. Simon immediately shut the engine down. Moments later, the pit crew was staring at several bent turbo blades.

The turbo problem wasn't the *Special*'s fault, of course. But that fact did little to cheer Vollstedt. He could see that the chances of his car being able to qualify were dwindling with each passing day. Had he been a superstitious man, he might have thought that the *Special* was jinxed.

Vollstedt kept looking at the calendar. The time for the qualification runs was fast approaching. They were scheduled for Saturday and Sunday, May 22 and 23, one week before the 500 rolled. He began to say that, if things didn't improve soon, he would have to pull the car out of competition and not waste everyone's time by trying to qualify.

On Friday, May 21, Vollstedt met with Janet and the crew. It was a sad group that assembled in the *Special's* garage in Gasoline Alley. Everyone knew that the past days of hard work hadn't given the car an extra ounce of power. It didn't have a hope of qualifying. There was only one thing left to do. Forget about the 500 for this year.

There were downcast eyes all around the big room. And slow, reluctant nods of agreement.

But—

Vollstedt looked at Janet sitting quietly on a workbench. He couldn't stand the idea that she was going to miss the chance of being the first woman to qualify for the 500. She'd worked so hard and performed so well since their first meeting at Ontario back in February. She'd certainly be able to qualify in a more powerful car —a car such as A. J. Foyt's *Coyote*. It was his backup car and, though he wouldn't be using it in the 500, it was here at Indy.

And so Vollstedt had an idea in mind.

Perhaps Foyt would lend the *Coyote* to Janet and give her the chance to hit a qualifying speed in it.

Vollstedt went to a telephone and called Foyt. When he returned a few minutes later, his lean face was brighter than it had been in days. Fine sportsman that Foyt was, he'd said that Janet should have every opportunity to see just how well she could do. He'd be glad to lend her the *Coyote*. She could take it out for a practice run on Sunday.

Happy shouts echoed through the garage. With the *Coyote*, Janet was sure to hit the 180 target. Then she could take the car into an actual qualification run. Her chances of being in the 500 were still very much alive.

Janet was as delighted as all the others. But she wasn't ready to give up on the *Special* just yet. She wanted to take it out for one more practice run on Saturday. Vollstedt agreed. No harm would be done and perhaps she could break the Paula Murphy speed record at the same time.

Janet replied that she really wasn't interested in the record. All she wanted to do was urge the *Special* up to within qualifying range. And so out the car went for what was to be its last run at Indy that year. Janet came nowhere near the needed 180 mph. But she did gun the car to well over 174 mph and came back as the new holder of the closed-course record for women.

At least, it was something she could take home from Indy if she failed to do well in Foyt's car.

For the rest of that Saturday, Janet watched the other

cars in the actual qualification runs. As usual, the speeds were fantastic. All were above 180 mph and some were even up at the 188 mark. She took a deep breath. Tomorrow, with luck, she'd be right there among those speeds. She was sure she could do it.

And that's exactly what Janet did do when she got behind the *Coyote's* wheel the next morning. She took a little time to acquaint herself with the car and then ran it up to a blazing 181 mph, holding it steadily in the groove the whole time. On returning to the pits, she was surrounded by jubilant friends. She'd easily gotten within qualifying range. She could do even better this afternoon in an actual qualification run. The many problems of the past days seemed to fade away . . .

But, suddenly, there was a new problem—one that took all the joy out of the moment.

Everyone had thought that Foyt, in lending the *Coyote* to Janet, had meant for her to qualify in it and then take it into the 500. But that turned out to be a misunderstanding. Or perhaps A.J. had changed his mind.

Whatever the case, Foyt was now shaking his head and saying that he had loaned the *Coyote* only for a practice run. He didn't want Janet to go on to the qualifications with it. He couldn't risk a possible accident because he was planning to use the car soon in another race.

Foyt explained that he had loaned the car just to see if Janet was good enough to hit a qualifying speed in a sufficiently powerful racer. He had wanted her to learn for herself just what she could do.

And how had she done? Terrific, Foyt said.

But he added that he had gone out on a limb in even risking the *Coyote* for some practice laps. He just didn't have all that many cars to risk.

All this was the worst news yet. It topped anything that had ever happened to the *Special*. There was just one ray of hope, however. At two o'clock Sunday afternoon, Foyt telephoned Janet to say that he was thinking things over and might change his mind. If he did, he would give her a call by five.

The rest of the afternoon passed slowly. Then five o'clock came. And went. Without the jangle of the telephone bell.

A numb and dejected Vollstedt team went out to dinner that evening. The conversation was quiet and no one seemed able to say very much. It just didn't seem possible that the Indy dream was ending this way. Janet left early and returned to her motel. She was exhausted by the tension of the day and needed a good night's sleep.

But she awoke suddenly at three o'clock in the morning. She stared up at the ceiling, and the disappointments of the past days—capped by today's shattering disappointment—hit her with full force. After trying so hard and putting up with so much controversy, she had come to the end of the Indy road in defeat.

She had made some history, yes. She had been the first woman to come to the 500. She had been the first woman to practice on the Indy track. She had taken the closed-course speed record for women. She had come within qualifying range and could have gone on to be in the race. And she had proved that women indeed had a place in championship cars and could handle them expertly. The world of big-car racing would never be the same again.

In themselves, these were triumphs that she could remember for a lifetime.

But the biggest prizes of all had escaped her. She hadn't gotten the chance to qualify. She hadn't made the great race. Later she was to say that, in the dark hours of the night, she could hardly bear those thoughts.

Soon, though, the disappointment passed and she began to think again like the experienced driver she was. She had lost before in her career. All she had done now was to miss the 500 this year.

If she had anything to say about it, there would be next year.

10

New Worlds to Conquer

No sooner had Janet lost her 500 chance than her life took one of its unexpected turns. She had been surprised so many times before in her career. There had been Gordon McKenzie suddenly advising her to enter racing. There had been Rolla Vollstedt calling out of the blue with the Indy offer. And now she was being surprised again, this time by a woman named Lynda Ferrari.

A bank vice-president in North Carolina, Lynda was a racing fan. She had followed Janet's Indy adventures with great admiration. But just recently, she had heard a local businessman snort that this Janet Guthrie really wasn't much of a driver. The remark had angered Lynda, and she had decided to do something about it.

Her chance came when Janet missed qualifying for the 500. Lynda flew to Indianapolis with an offer. She said she would sponsor Janet in the World 600 stock car race. It was to be held on May 30, the very same day that the 500 rolled.

As had happened when Vollstedt had first called months ago, Janet was speechless. If there was one thing she hadn't been thinking about, it was a race sponsored by the National Association for Stock Car Auto Racing. She had never driven in NASCAR competition. She had never handled a stock car.

But the offer was a real challenge. And it helped to make up for the Indy disappointment. Janet nodded happily. She'd love to try for the race.

And so, while Johnny Rutherford, A. J. Foyt, and all the other qualifiers practiced for the 500, Janet flew to Charlotte, North Carolina, where the 600 was to be run. Ahead was a week of getting acquainted with a new car, a new track, and a new style of racing.

Ahead also was a week of criticism. It was the same sort she had heard at Trenton and Indy, only now the name of the car was changed. Janet Guthrie had no business in a stock car. She wasn't strong enough to handle one of the big, 3,500-pound jobs. She didn't have enough experience. Who did she think she was to try for the classic 600 without first competing in less-important races?

As at Indy, Janet took the criticism quietly. More important, she began to silence it by doing well at Charlotte. Driving a Chevrolet that A. J. Foyt had once piloted, she circled the track at 152.797 mph on Thursday, May 27, to qualify for the race. It was the twelfth fastest speed recorded that particular day, and it won her the twenty-seventh pole position in the forty-car field.

She had missed qualifying for the 500. But now she

became the first woman ever to qualify for a major event —a Grand National Speedway event, it was called— sponsored by NASCAR.

Then it was Sunday, May 30. Out in Indianapolis, Johnny Rutherford hurtled through the rain to take the 500, with A. J. Foyt coming in second and Gordon Johncock following in the third spot. Dick Simon, driving a Vollstedt car, finished in thirty-second place. At Charlotte, Janet was up against a humid day that sent the track temperature soaring to 130 degrees.

The race started tamely enough. There were a few caution flags for minor spin-outs. Several cars dropped out with smoking engines. But then things became as sizzling as the weather. Dave Marcis, running in fourth place, spun his Dodge on a turn during lap 232. Buddy Baker was right behind him in a Ford and had to sail into the wall to avoid a broadside crash. Both cars, their drivers uninjured, were done for the day.

On lap 301, David Pearson and his Wood Brothers Mercury grabbed the lead. Trailing by seven seconds and pushing hard to close the gap was Dodge driver Richard Petty. The finish promised to be a close one until, with just two laps to go, there was another accident. Grant Adcox and James Hylton collided on a turn and slithered all over the track. The seventh caution flag of the day came out.

All cars held position and the flag was still out when Pearson shot across the finish line for the win.

And what of Janet? She was far back in the pack— twenty-one laps behind Pearson—when the 600 ended.

But she was anything but unhappy with her first appearance in NASCAR competition. Driving in a brand new world to her, she had placed fifteenth and had stayed in there for the entire run. Twenty-three cars and their drivers had been forced to give up along the way.

But best of all, in reaching the fifteenth spot, she had worked her way past twelve cars from her twenty-seventh pole position. Janet's performance won her the Curtis Turner Award for achievement in the race.

After such a good beginning, Janet moved on to other NASCAR races. In June 1976 she drove her Chevrolet in the Firecracker 400 at Daytona Beach, the scene of so many of the triumphs with the Macmillan Motor Maids. Cale Yarborough took the race. David Pearson came in second, and Bobby Allison third. Janet placed fifteenth.

Then in February 1977 she improved her placement, coming in twelfth in the Richmond 400 at the Virginia State Fairgrounds. It was the highest spot taken by a rookie that day. Again, Cale Yarborough led the field. Darrell Waltrip ran second, with Benny Parsons right behind him.

Though it was fun learning this world of NASCAR racing, Janet could not forget the Indy disappointment. She was determined to go on racing for Rolla Vollstedt, who had given her the biggest break of her life. And she was determined to be on hand when the time came for the 1977 500. Indy. That was the world she really wanted to conquer.

Janet and Vollstedt began to race early in preparation for the coming 500. But, in a June 1976 appearance, their luck seemed no better than at Indy. From the very start of the Schaefer 500 at Pocono, Pennsylvania, the car had Janet in trouble. Nine times she was forced to the pits for repairs. Then, on the eighty-ninth lap, the transmission failed and refused to hold the car in fourth gear.

Despite the poor showing, Vollstedt was able to smile broadly in early 1977. He told Janet that he had obtained a fine racer for the 500, one that surely wouldn't be as plagued by trouble as the *Special*. In fact, it was one of the greatest cars around—the *Lindsey Hopkins Lightning*. Roger McCluskey had tested it recently at the Brickyard and—get this!—it had hit an amazing 198.7 mph.

The news delighted Janet, as did the car when she drove it for the first time. On February 8 she and Vollstedt announced that they would once again try for the 500. Janet told the assembled reporters that she had the greatest confidence in the *Lightning* and that there was no finer racing team than Rolla's. She added that she was looking forward to working with her big-car teacher —Dick Simon—and learning more and more from him.

As for Simon, he was sure of one thing now that Janet had a truly high-powered and trouble-free car:

"You'll see that girl up front this year."

Simon was right. As soon as Janet arrived in Indianapolis for the 1977 race, she made her presence felt. She posted the fastest speed—185.6 mph—of any driver who went out on the track the first day of practice.

73

Then, in the next days, she did just as well and even better, hitting speeds of 183, 186, and 191 mph.

But she was due for trouble. On May 10, when coming through a curve, the *Lightning* rode up too high and smacked the concrete wall. The Vollstedt pit crew watched with clenched teeth as the car slithered along the track and the sound of the crash echoed across the infield. There was a sigh of relief when Janet was found unhurt and the car not badly damaged.

A week of fine tuning and testing by Dick Simon brought the racer back up to good speeds. On Sunday, May 22, it was ready for a qualification run. Face set and determined, Janet climbed into the cockpit. Today, she had the chance to even the score for last year's disappointment. Today, if she had anything to say about it, she was going to become the first woman to qualify for the classic 500.

Once more, the speed for qualifying had to be well above the 180 mark. Smoothly, Janet circled the track, warming the *Lightning*. Then it was time for the qualifying laps—four in all.

On the first lap, she hit 187.500. The second saw her up to 188.363. She swept through the third at 188.798. And the fourth at 188.957.

Triumphantly, Janet shut down the engine and glided into the pit area. Her smile was wide as Vollstedt, the crew, newsmen, and photographers crowded round the green-and-white *Lightning*. All of last year's disappointment was erased. She'd done it!

After fifteen long years in racing, this quiet and determined woman had won a spot in the 500.

The next moment of triumph came on Sunday, May 29, when the voice of Tony Hulman, the president of the Indianapolis Motor Speedway, was heard on the track's public address system. For the first time in the history of the 500, a different order to start the race was given.

The 300,000 spectators broke into a roar as Hulman announced, "In company with the first lady ever to qualify for Indianapolis, gentlemen, start your engines."

But the race itself was to be a disappointment for Janet. She ran well in the thirty-three-car field for a few laps. Then her engine began to sputter. Into the pits she came for the first of eight stops. Quick adjustments were made, only to be followed by valve trouble moments later.

On her second stop, the fuel mixture of alcohol and methanol expanded in the heat of the day and spilled into the cockpit as she was sitting there. It seeped through her driving suit and burned her skin painfully. She climbed out and was surrounded by a fire crew. Their extinguishers were aimed and ready should the suit burst into flames.

The valve was replaced. Janet shot back out onto the track. But now there was ignition trouble—trouble that took an hour and a new ignition system to repair. Then other problems followed. They all refused to be corrected. At last, Vollstedt and the crew had to admit that Janet's big day at Indianapolis was done.

75

She nodded and started back to the garage in Gasoline Alley to remove her soaked driving suit. She had completed just twenty-seven laps. By day's end, the *Lightning* would be given twenty-ninth place in the field of thirty-three, and A. J. Foyt would streak across the finish line to become the first four-time winner at Indianapolis.

But, though she hadn't done well in the 500, Janet knew that she'd won the respect of racing fans everywhere. The roar of an appreciative crowd echoed in her ears all during the long walk to Gasoline Alley.

With her second Indy attempt behind her, Janet could look back on a career that any driver—man or woman—would be more than proud to have. She had competed in sports cars, championship cars, and stock cars—the "big three" of racing. And, despite disappointments and defeats along the way, she had competed in them all with great success.

But it was a career that was far from over. There would be many more races as she continued to prove that women definitely have a place in the most high-powered of cars.

There was no telling what new challenges lay ahead. But everyone could be sure of one thing. Whatever those challenges turned out to be, Janet Guthrie would meet them with determination, coolness, and intelligence.

That's how she does things.

Index

Edward F. Dolan, Jr. and Richard B. Lyttle have been close friends for ten years. Both are native Californians and each has written several books. The Signal Books mark their first efforts as co-authors.

Mr. Lyttle was raised in Ojai, served in the Navy during World War II, and attended the University of California at Berkeley. He has worked as a cowboy, farmer, newspaper reporter, and editor. He began selling stories and articles for children in the 1950s.

Mr. Dolan's boyhood was spent in Los Angeles. After serving with the 101st Airborne Division during World War II, he attended the University of San Francisco. He began writing when he was in his teens and has also been a teacher and a newspaper reporter.

The two men met while they were reporters for rival newspapers in northern California. Both are avid sportsmen. Mr. Lyttle beats his co-author regularly at golf. But Mr. Dolan says he can outswim Mr. Lyttle any day of the week.

Mr. Lyttle and his wife, Jean, live in Point Reyes Station, a small town north of San Francisco. Mr. Dolan and his wife, Rose, live nearby in the town of Novato.